St. Peter's Fiesta

THROUGH THE YEARS

ACKNOWLEDGMENTS

Many people contributed to the making of this book. People with a sense of love, of family, and of tradition. We would like to express our appreciation to those people, without whose efforts this book would never have been possible. So many have contributed their family photos and stories, that we must apologize for any names that have inadvertantly been left off this list.

—Jamey Burnham
Joe Palmisano

The St. Peter's Fiesta Committee for their financial contribution

Gloucester Bank & Trust
Gloucester Waterfront League
The Gloucester Daily Times
Cape Ann Historical Society
Saint Peter's Club

Sara Day
Phil Salzman
Kathy Roberts
Bart Piscitello
Charlie Lowe
Rick Lowe
Ronnie Goulart
Marc Verga
Tom Favazza
James Verga
Vito Piscitello
Mike Randazza
Sam Ciaramitaro
Anthony Suputo
Andy Orlando
Joe & Joan Ciolino
David Marsh
Mary Wessling
Mike & Nina Calomo

Jerry Ciolino
Lou Biondo
Mitch McGillivary
Lucia Amaro
Rosie & James Verga
Sara Favazza
Agnes Burnham
Jamey Burnham
Stephanie LoGrande
Ed Wall
Joe Morrissey
Joe & Rose Agrusso
Paul Nicastro
Joe Marino
Grace Favazza
Eric Loicano
Mary Interrante
Leo Sabato
Mike & Phyllis Orlando
Jerry Goulart
Lena Novello
Bob Puglisi
Nina Conti
Celia Dousette
Gaye Catanina
James Ryan
Conchetta Gruppo
Dominic Sanfilippo
David Leeco
Benny Favazza

Nina Francis
Mike Favazza
Mary Scola
Joe Giagalone
Grace Favazza
The Ciluffo Family
Desi Smith
Charlie Palmisano
Joe Palmisano
Frank Frontiero
Joeseph McCormack
Jack Lombardo
Vincent Orlando
Dom Nicastro
Eric Loicano
Cathy Palmisano
Michael Linquata
Sonny and John Deltorchio
Erica McDonald
Josephine Maniscaco
The Matarazzo Family
Meredith Fine
Bikie Scola
Patsy Frontierro
Busty Palozzola
Lenny Billante
Anne Linquata
Louis Linquata
The Linquata Family
The Favazza Family

Copyright © 2001 by
The Young Men's Coalition

All rights reserved. No part of this book may be reproduced in any form without written permission of the copyright owners. All images in this book have been reproduced with the knowledge and prior consent of the persons concerned and no responsibility is accepted by producer, publisher, or printer for any infringement of copyright or otherwise, arising from the contents of this publication. Every effort has been made to ensure that credits accurately comply with information supplied.

ISBN 0-9710178-0-8

10 9 8 7 6 5 4 3 2 1

Book design by
Sara Day / SYP Design & Production
http://www.sypdesign.com

Printed in Korea

Photo courtesy of Cape Ann Historical Society

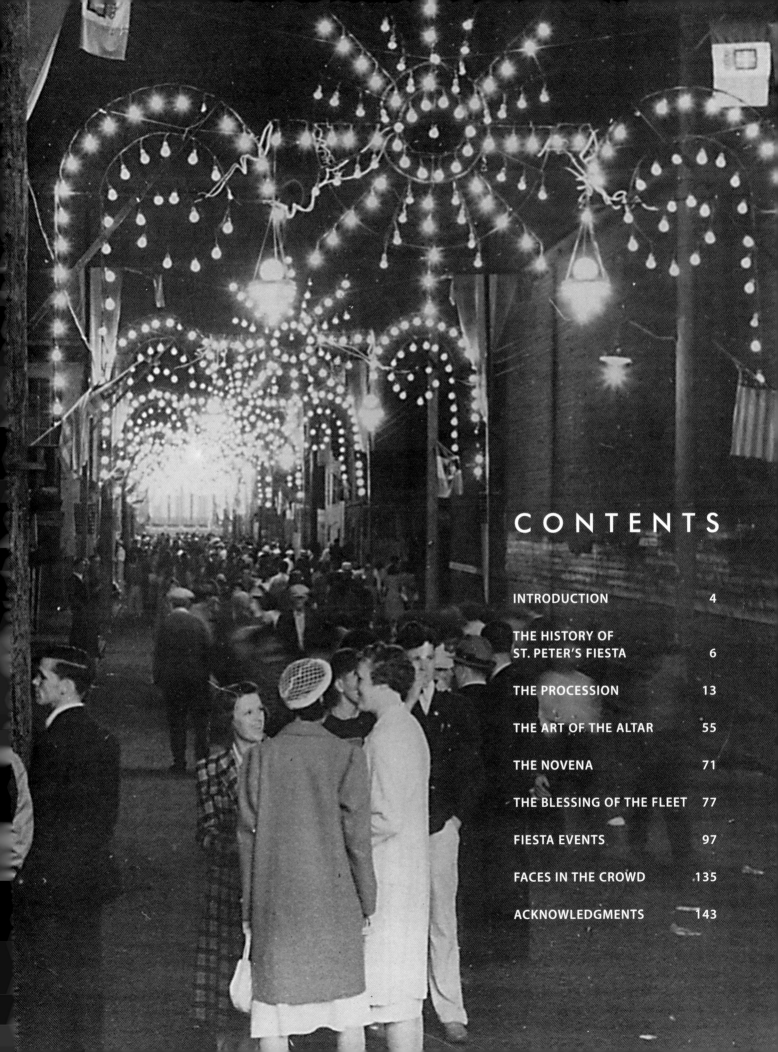

CONTENTS

INTRODUCTION	4
THE HISTORY OF ST. PETER'S FIESTA	6
THE PROCESSION	13
THE ART OF THE ALTAR	55
THE NOVENA	71
THE BLESSING OF THE FLEET	77
FIESTA EVENTS	97
FACES IN THE CROWD	135
ACKNOWLEDGMENTS	143

INTRODUCTION

Sometimes it seems the world is moving so fast that by the time we grasp a new idea or trend, it's already gone. In our generation's quest to "get ahead," important values sometimes get left behind. Values like family, and community—and tradition.

The past seven decades have seen many changes, yet one tradition has remained steadfastly. The St. Peter's Fiesta, held in Gloucester, Massachusetts, is a time-honored tradition whose significance has been passed on in this community from generation to generation. It is a four-day summer celebration in honor of St. Peter, the patron saint of the fishermen.

Gloucester fishermen lived and worked by a different calendar than most. Birthdays, school plays, and holidays were missed during the year simply because the weather was good and there was no guarantee it would last—especially in New England. But every year, for four days starting on the last Thursday of June, you could be sure the fleet would be in for Fiesta. It was a time to rest up, to clean, paint and make repairs—to celebrate and to count our many blessings.

Gloucester is a town rich in ethnicity, and the Sicilian and Portuguese communities both add much to the color of this unique place. For over seventy years, the St. Peter's Fiesta has been a time to honor these hardworking communities, through recognition, prayer, and celebration.

When viewing this photo journal, it is important to appreciate the tremendous amounts of hard work and dedication required by this community to bring us, year after year, beautiful parade floats, ornate altars, creative greasy-pole costumes, and exciting boat races.

Fiesta, like the rest of our nation, has been challenged by the turmoil of war, changing political views, and economic woes. Yet it's message of honoring heritage, community, and family remain clear. It is a message shouted through the streets of Gloucester each summer: *Viva, San Pietro!* Long live, St. Peter!

It is our hope that *St. Peter's Fiesta Through the Years*, helps to recognize the importance of our heritage—to embrace it, to teach it, and to preserve it for our children.

—Sara Day
granddaughter of Salvatore Favazza

Salvatore Favazza poses with his wife Maria in front of the altar in 1948. His gesture of attaining the statue of the patron saint of the fishermen and parading it through the streets of his small neighborhood, later grew into a four-day tradition celebrated by fishermen, townspeople, and tourists alike.

THE HISTORY OF ST. PETER'S FIESTA

The pride of a community steeped in tradition rests on the shoulders of its members. The families of Gloucester's fishing fleet have honored St. Peter through the years, giving thanks for his protection and his compassion for those who make their living on the sea. Large, and beautifully-ornate altars were constructed to house the statue for the four-day celebration, with room enough for a bandstand.

The St. Peter's Fiesta, like the many Italian religious feasts celebrated in Boston's North End, originated from Sicilian culture. A people of strong religious convictions, they honored many patron saints with festivals of food, parades, music, and prayer.

The late Captain Salvatore Favazza came to the United States from Favoratta, Sicily, first settling in Detroit—working and saving to bring the rest of his family to America. While working on railroads, and then later, peddling fruit, he had heard of a small, sea-side town in Massachusetts that had the look and feel of his home in Favoratta. He would make Gloucester, Massachusetts, his new home and together, with his wife, Maria, raise a family of 10 children, while making his living as a sea captain. As a gesture of gratitude for his many blessings, Captain Favazza thought it only fitting to give thanks to the patron saint of the fishermen, St. Peter, as was done in the old country.

He commissioned a Charlestown sculptor to create the statue of St. Peter in 1926, and brought it to Gloucester, where it was kept in a storefront window. Neighbors hailed the arrival of the statue with a novena (nine days of prayer), for protection and good fortune from the sea. They danced to music that was provided by a simple band of only an accordion and a mandolin. So that all families could participate in honoring the saint, the statue was mounted to a platform and paraded through the narrow streets of the predominantly Sicilian neighborhood known as "The Fort." People would decorate their homes along the route by hanging beautiful quilts and bedspreads from windows overhead. As the procession passed by, the fishermen in the streets below would shout: *"Me chi samiou, duté*

This photo, dated 1927, is said to be one of the first Fiestas on record. The statue of St. Peter, adorned with beautifully hand-made decorations, was paraded through the narrow streets of Gloucester's predominantly Sicilian neighborhood known as "The Fort." People along the route would decorate their homes for the festival by hanging brightly-colored quilts from windows overhead. Here, the crowd stops momentarily to hear a brief poem about their patron saint recited by a fisherman's wife. The man standing in front of the statue, just behind the woman holding the bouquet of flowers, is Salvatore Favazza, founder of the Fiesta. In the far lower left-hand corner of the photo is his baby daughter Mary. Years later, the woman reciting the poem would become Mary's mother-in-law.

muté? Viva San Pietro!" Translated: "Shout it louder, are we all mute? Long live St. Peter!"

As the festival gained popularity, a committee was formed to work with the City of Gloucester to handle the many details of the Fiesta. Italian fishermen would donate a percent of their catch to a Fiesta fund. Donations are also collected along the parade route and pinned to long ribbons that cascade from the statue of St. Peter.

Today, the Fiesta Committee is integral in assuring smooth sailing for the many events of the Fiesta. The official celebration begins with the procession of St. Peter at midnight from the St. Peter's Club to the altar in St. Peter's Square. The following days are comprised of concerts, Seine Boat Races, the famous Greasy-Pole contest, an outdoor Mass in front of the altar, a parade, and the blessing of the fleet. These events are interspersed with carnival rides and games for the children, and vendors selling everything from italian sausage, to lemon ice.

The Fiesta ends as it begins, with a procession that takes the statue of St. Peter back to his place in the window of the St. Peter's Club on Main Street. There he will take his place for another year, much like he did in the tiny storefront window years ago, with only an accordion and a mandolin. Another Fiesta come and gone, another cycle—complete.

The St. Peter's Fiesta Committee is responsible for organizing the many details of the festival. Pictured above is one of the first committees from 1932, including (top, left to right): Louis Pascucci, John Grillo, Leonard Linguata (bottom, left to right): Gaspar Contrino, Ben Curcuru, Peter Favazza, and John Chincola.

At left is the current Fiesta Committee. Left to right are: (back row) Joe Novello, Anthony Cusamano, Michael Linquata, Al Milifolge,; (center row) Nino Cotone, Anthony Giacalone, Antonio Parisi, Leo Vitale, Sam Ferra, Rose Ailleo; (front row) Father Guthrie, Tom Brancleone, The Most Reverent Bishop Francis X. Irwin, Santo Millitello.

Photo courtesy of Gloucester Daily Times

A seine boat makes the crucial turn around the flag that marks the half-way point of this excruciating mile-long race. The crews of three boats—Nina, Pinta, and Santa Maria—take their rowing very seriously, dedicating long hours of practice, rain or shine. Onlookers flock to Pavillion Beach with binoculars and enthusiasm to watch the traditional "Seine Boat Races" that have become an integral part of St. Peter's Fiesta events.

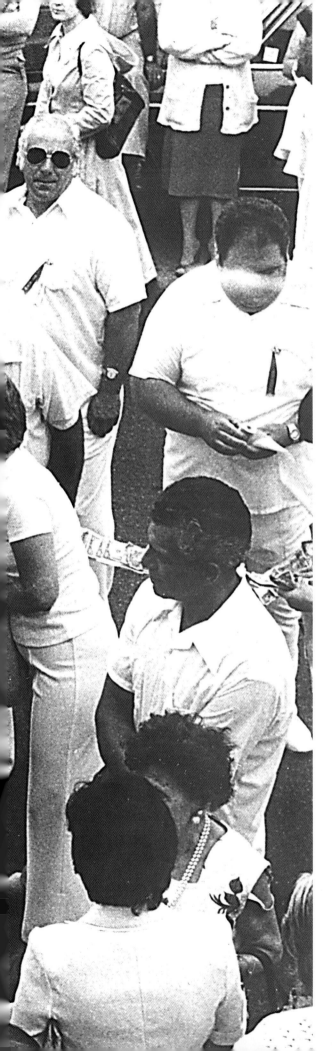

THE PROCESSION

WHAT BEGAN as a small neighborhood procession has evolved into a grand, two-mile-long parade through the streets of Gloucester. Children dress in beautiful hand-made costumes depicting religious icons, angels, and saints. Elaborate floats are pulled by flatbed trucks decorated with hundreds of tissue-paper flowers. Marching bands step lively, along with politicians and dignitaries, the fiesta committee, and the 700-pound statue of St. Peter, carried on the shoulders of Gloucester fishermen

THE MEANING OF THE FIESTA

The Saint Peter's Fiesta has gone through some physical changes since its small, backyard beginning. Today it is a publicized and public event that caters to a wider audience. However, to those who have a personal affection for the celebration, it remains an aspect of the unity that is contained in the word *community*.

The Fiesta is a time of celebration and thanksgiving, and also of renewal. A time to renew the friendships and camaraderie of people who share a common thread, bringing them together as a community in prayer and socialization.

For the people of Gloucester, Fiesta is a priority that requires almost as much preparation as Christmas. For this community, and those who grew up here but later moved away, Fiesta remains more than simply four days of summer.

People who have never been involved in the fishing industry, or know personally of anyone who is, come to the Fiesta to be a part of that deep sense of community.

Things are so much different than in the earliest years of the festivities. It seems there are as many carnies barking out come-ons, as there are people speaking Sicilian. The carnival rides at times are pushed so close to the stage it sometimes becomes a distraction to the traditional entertainment. To some, the Fiesta will no doubt remain just a carnival. And although the carnival attractions bring in money that supports the four-day celebration year after year, those who grew up with the St. Peter's Fiesta—who have the spirit of the Fiesta in their hearts—know it isn't about rides and games of chance.

These early photos from the 1930s show the proceession marching through archways of lights and flags of "The Fort" section of Gloucester.

The community of St. Peter is the people who are thankful for a chance to spend a warm evening with friends and relatives. It is those who set aside time to attend every night of the novena, and those who put together the floats for the parade, because it's been a family tradition. It is those who carry the statute on their shoulder mile after mile because they been taught it is an honor, and those who are no longer involved in the fishing industry but still believe that St. Peter watches over them and their families.

Above, ladies march past the old Cape Ann Market on Washington Street. The St. Peter's Auxilliary poses in front of the altar.

Captain Favazza leads white gloved fishermen in this early Fiesta photo.

THE PROCESSION

Above, the procession continues along Prospect Street toward St. Ann's Church.

Below women march past the old Birdseye Building at the corner of Commercial Street and Commercial Court.

In this 1957 photo, St. Peter is carried past the Amvets Club on Prospect Street (from left to right) Tony Palmisano, Johnny Parisi, Sam Tally Nicastro, Sam Lopicolo, Steve D'Amico, Capt. Salvatore Favazza, Leo Sabato, and Cons Parisi.

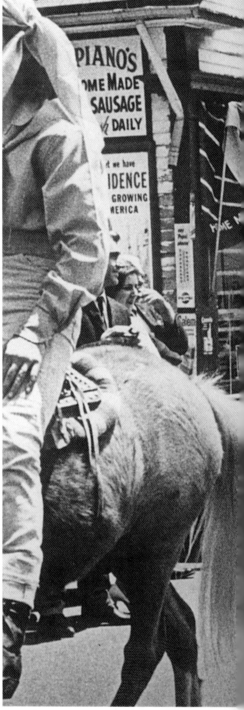

Above, a flatbed truck carries a detailed model of the St. Ann's Church, whose congregation consists mostly of Italian-Americans.

Below, a marching band entertains the crowds along Main Street.

An authentic Sicilian donkey cart rolls along Washington Street, past Cher-Ami Ice Cream Shop, and Trupiano's Superette. Trupiano's Superette is still in business today.

The community of St. Peter is also the people who go to Pavilion Beach to cheer on the greasy-pole walkers and talk about the styles of past champions—knowing first hand because those champions are still personal friends—and about which seine boat crew was the greatest of all time, and taking pride in the fact that they were once part of the crews that pulled the great oars.

But most of all it's about the people who stay to the very end of the Fiesta on Sunday evening, even though most will have to be at work early in the morning. They stay right to the time when St. Peter is brought around the Fort, continuing a tradition that started when the neighborhood was filled with those who depended on the sea for a living. Even as St. Peter looks heavenward, he no longer sees the festive lights that use to span the entire route, he can still hear the people calling his name. He can still feel the confetti thrown from the few remaining long-time Fort families, that have been doing it for a lot more years than most of those walking have been alive.

Cardinal Richard Cushing poses with Salvatore J. Favazza and Anita Frontiero.

Below, veterans Nat Misuraca (center) and Peter Favazza (far right).

Opposite, returning World War II Veterans march in the St. Peter's Parade of 1946.

A happy fishing crew is followed by a costumed St. Peter.

Below, in earlier years of Fiesta, the statue was carried to St. Ann's Church for prayer.

Pictured in front of the Statue of St. Peter from left to right are Tony Palmisano, Capt. Salvatore Favazza, Sophia Favaloro, and Salvatore Pussiteri.

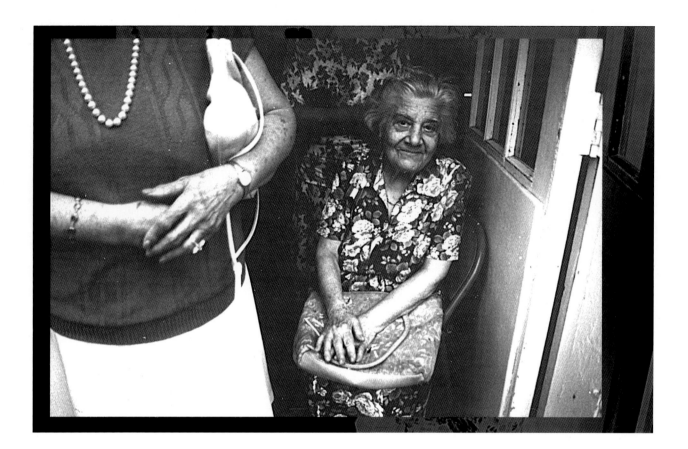

Isabella DiGirolimo enjoys the festivities from the Mother of Grace Club on Washington Street.

Opposite, members of the Fiesta Committee prepare the statue of St. Peter for the procession.

> The community of the St. Peter's Fiesta is the faces of the people and seeing in those the faces their mothers and fathers, and their grandparents when they use to make the pilgrimage. It's seeing these people walking and carrying their children, teaching this newer generation the traditions and true meaning of what these past four days signify to the family of St. Peter. And hoping that their children will pass these traditions along to the next generation and generations to come.
>
> —JJ Favazza

Posing for a Fiesta photo are (above, from left to right), Sam Frontiero, Sam Verga, "Busty" Saputo, and Jim Verga, (below) Cecelia Kyrouz, Grace Ann Parisi, and Gracia di Maria in 1958.

Opposite, young girls in white carry baskets of flowers led by a angel along Prospect Street.

THE PROCESSION

A classic car cruises along in this 1958 photo. Driving is Joseph (Pino) Scola, with his father, Sam in the passenger seat. In the backseat is his uncle Louie Linquata and grandfather, Sam Frontiero.

With decorated fishing boats docked in the background, Captain Favazza leads the procession during Fiesta of 1958. Pictured are (left to right) Ambrose Parisi, Tom Parisi, Salvatore Favazza, John Parisi, Tony Palmisano, Ed Tocco, Salvatore Nicastro, Leo Sabato, and Katie Linquata.

St. Peter is returned to the altar after this parade of 1950. Carrying the sign are (left to right) Philip Parisi, Cathy Palmisano, Sal Scola, Marie Scola and Cons Parisi.

Opposite, Albina Gentile Anthony Giacalone depicts the Prince of Peace in 1963.

Above, parade remnants in front of the Mother of Grace Club on Washington Street.

Left, a pose from an era gone by, left to right is Mary Scola, Pimie Biondo, Catherine and Joseph Rallo, and Dulie Palmisano.

Opposite, John Parisi guides the statue in 1970's.

36 ST. PETER'S FIESTA THROUGH THE YEARS

Above, part of their heritage, a colorful Sicilian cart rolls along the parade route in 1960.

Opposite, little angels grace the parade. Top are Kay Verga (Ahern) and Marylou Burnham in 1965.

Over the years the Fiesta parade has seen many dignitaries and politicians. Above, a young Ted Kennedy marches in the parade of 1962.

Left, John Parisi, who led the procession of St. Peter after the passing of Capt. Favazza, is showered with confetti in June of 1985.

A young woman depicts Our Lady of Good Voyage, who holds a fishing vessel in her hand. The actual statue stands high atop the church of the same name in the Portugese section of Gloucester. The architecture of the church, with it's double blue towers, is a prominent part of the Gloucester skyline.

Above, a float depicts Jesus handing St. Peter the keys to the Kingdom of Heaven.

Below, from left to right, Joe Scola, Larry Biondo, and Joe Palmisano march with the banner of flowers introducing St. Peter.

Opposite, the saint is honored with an elaborate float by the St. Peter's Women's Auxiliary.

Left, Jamie Burnham and Jim Ciarametaro march in front of Leanne Ciarametaro and Francine Giamanco in 1966.

Below, Matthew Martin and Elizabeth Burnham (daughter of Jamie, above) march in a the Fiesta parade of 2000.

Above, John Palmisano and Maria Biondo Martin along with Michael and Tom Abbot carry the banner announcing the 50th anniversary of the Fiesta.

Right, Pearl Parisi attaches donations to ribbons that cascade from the statue.

THE PROCESSION

Photo courtesy of Gloucester Daily Times

Above, Cardinal Bernard Law visits the Fiesta in 1987.

Left, Fiesta Committee members in 1981 (from left to right) Nino Sanfilippo, Mike Diliberti, Santo Militello, Al Milfoge, Sam Linquata, Sam Militello, and Busty Mocerri.

On the previous pages, Sicilian and Portugese communities of Gloucester unite, honoring both St. Peter and Our Lady of Good Voyage.

Left, Jesus is portrayed guarded by a Roman soldier.

Below, young boys of the Novello family depict fishermen on the sea of Gallilea.

Above, a crew of young sailors is watched over by Our Lady of Good Voyage.

Right, a beautifully crowned St. Mary of Trapani.

Even the most honorable guards can grow weary during the parade.

Opposite, Peter Favazza is in elaborate costume, depicting St. Peter in 1963.

Above, young girls march in religious costume.

Left, Ann deCruz accompanies a float depicting the Assumption of Mary.

Opposite, draped in satin this float is adorned with beautiful patron saints.

THE ART OF THE ALTAR

LARGE CROWDS attending St. Peter's Fiesta necessitated the construction of elaborate, outdoor altars that would serve as a focal point for the celebration. The firm of Emilio Matarazzo Inc. served for many years as the Fiesta's official decorator. Matarazzo and his sons would string colorful lights up and down Commercial Street, and construct an ornate altar that would house the statue of St. Peter. In later years, the altar would host large crowds attending the outdoor Mass. Each altar would vary in size and design, all resembling altars of famous churches in Italy, Sicily, and Greece. The present-day altar was constructed in 1985 and has additional room for Fiesta concert bands and entertainers.

THE MASTER

Emilo Matarazzo was considered by most to be an artist of exact in detail. A designer who specialized in festival work, Matarazzo was proud of the fact that he pursued this unique art form that had been passed down from his forefathers in his home country of Naples, Italy.

Emilo along with his sons Tony, Rudy, Sonny, and Eddie, would work in a warehouse in the Chinatown section of Boston during the winter months, designing and constructing facades of cathedrals from Sicily, Italy, and Greece. Some of these creations were 65 feet in height and 45 feet long. They included bandstands which set back some 16 feet deep. In creating these altars the Matarazzo's would sometimes use up to 700 yards of cloth, 345 pounds of paper and foil, and 90 pounds of common pins. The paper and foil was cut entirely by hand, forming a detailed design that was later pined to the fabric. Sections of fabric and foil were joined together and along with some 9000 lights, a magnificent and colorful cathedral facade was created.

Above, this altar from 1935 boasts perfect symmetry and fine detail.

Opposite, one of the first Fiesta altars, this was built to sit directly on the ground. Steps to a higher platform were added in later years for the crowds to view entertainment and the Sunday Mass.

Emilio Matarazzo created some of the most beautiful altars in the earlier years of the Fiesta. Designs were based on architecture of churches in Sicily, Italy, and Greece.

Right, an altar displays dramatic lighting for a festive evening celebration.

Opposite, early altars were built in front of a house on Beach Court. Later, the altar was moved to its present positon in St. Peter's Square.

THE ART OF THE ALTAR 61

As the St. Peter's Fiesta grew in popularity, the altars became larger and more ornate, Emilio Matarazzo successfully met each creative challenge.

Opposite, the photo of this altar was dated 1935.

THE ART OF THE ALTAR

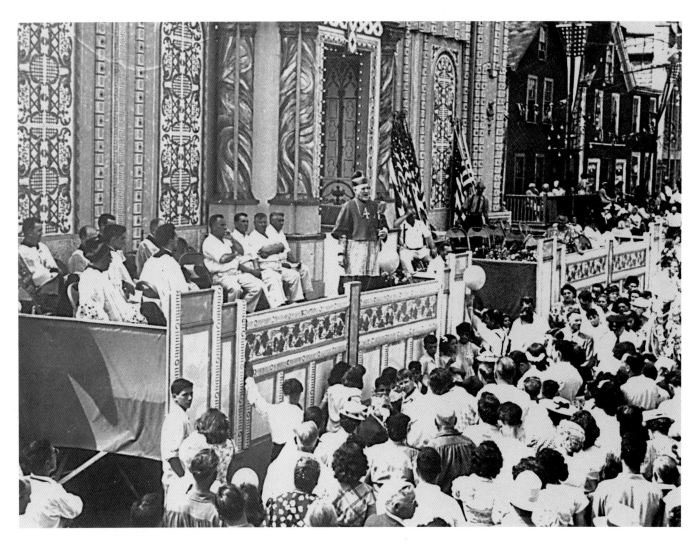

Cardinal Cushing, Archbishop of Boston, addressed the crowd from the altar in the 1940s. The photo of the altar at left is dated 1951.

The altar with bandstand in 1946.

This 1948 photo shows the painstaking detail of this lost art. Pictured from left to right: Louis Linquata, Captain Salvatore Favazza, his wife, Maria Favazza, and Nina Randazza.

Opposite, in this photo dated 1958, the altar is decorated with flowers and lights.

Above, Santo Militello, president of the St. Peter's Fiesta Committee in 1992.

Opposite, top, a priest addresses the crowd from the enormous altar of 1962. Bottom, the altar in 1968.

THE ART OF THE ALTAR 69

THE NOVENA

WHEN CAPTAIN SALVATORE FAVAZZA brought his magnificent statue of St. Peter home to Gloucester in 1927, his family and neighbors were moved to mark the occasion in one of the oldest and most traditional manners known to Roman Catholics. They began a novena—nine days of prayer, scriptural readings, and singing to honor the saint.

Photo courtesy of Gloucester Daily Times

NINE DAYS OF PRAYER

Since many families were involved in the local fishing industry, it was only appropriate for them to honor St. Peter, who was once a fisherman himself. Their novena to St. Peter included prayers of protection on the often treacherous waters off Cape Ann.

The early novena altars were designed and constructed by the wives of the fishermen. Though small in size, the altars were proudly decorated with the very best of what each family could afford. Finely embroidered tablecloths, normally reserved for family weddings and christenings, were hung behind and around the statue. Gold jewelry was hung from the hand of St. Peter as a symbolic gesture of their own personal committment. Heavy silk linens formed a skirt around the altar base, and flowers gathered from neighborhood gardens adorned the entire setting.

As the Fiesta grew in size and popularity, the novena became less important. The very purpose of the St. Peter's Fiesta—to give praise and thanks for good fortune and protection— was becoming lost in it's revelry. In the late 1970's, a group of determined women decided it was time to refocus on the purpose of the St. Peter's Fiesta. The novena was revived with great success. Today, men, women, and children attend the novena services in large numbers and stay for a social hour to enjoy coffee and pastries. Each year, the novena is held at the St. Peter's Club, and is open to the public.

Flowers from neighborhood gardens, and fine silks and linens adorn this homemade altar. The novena is held for eight days preceding the Fiesta.

Opposite, Mary Russo, Phyllis Quince, and Mrs. Milone join in prayer.

The Mother of Grace Club is made up of Gloucester women of deep religious conviction. Here, a dignitary from the Catholic church visits their altar and blesses members.

Opposite, Mary Favalora and Jennie Verga in prayer.

Photo courtesy of Gloucester Daily Times

THE BLESSING OF THE FLEET

ONE OF THE MOST important religious aspects of the St. Peter's Fiesta is The Blessing of the Fleet. One of the first blessings took place in 1945, celebrated by the Portuguese community. They marched from Our Lady of Good Voyage Church to the State Fish Pier where Archbishop Richard J. Cushing blessed the gathered fishing vessels. During the mid-1950s the Italian community joined the ceremony and gradually incorporated the blessing into Fiesta activities. Today the Blessing of the Fleet takes place on Stacy Boulevard near the Fisherman's Memorial. Visiting cardinals and bishops address the crowd, fishing boats, and pleasure craft blessing "all these ships and those who sail thereon" in a desire to ensure their safety and continued prosperity.

Photo courtesy of Gloucester Daily Times

BONAVENTURE

Throughout the years, the fishermen of Gloucester have seen much progression in the making and maintainence of their vessels. Wooden hulled vessels were replaced by stronger steel hulls and new modern electronic equipment was introduced, providing the opportunity for a more efficient and safer fleet. Yet no fishing vessel seemed complete without its annual blessing at the Fiesta. The Fiesta originated from fishing families that gathered together in prayer for the well being of their men at sea. Today, in this age of technology, fishing families still partake in the blessing, finding comfort in the deep religious belief that St. Peter, the patron saint of fishermen, watches over them.

The Gloucester fishing fleet has dwindled to a fraction of its original size, yet still gathers in the harbor, now along with recreational vessels, to receive its blessing.

Some fishermen, frustrated by low pay and strict government regulations, have unfortunately had to turn to other occupations. Others have stayed on. But whether or not a Gloucester fisherman remains upon the sea, he will always be a Gloucester fisherman. It is not what he does, it is what he is.

Above, crowds gather in front of the Fisherman's Memorial, and boats converge in the inner harbor for the blessing.

This 1956 photo, a banquet is held at the State Armory for the blessing of a fleet that was much larger and more lucrative than today's.

THE BLESSING OF THE FLEET

Above, the blessing is performed from a fishing vessel. Left, freshly painted vessels are decorated with colorful signal flags.

Photo courtesy of Gloucester Daily Times

Four of a fleet that at one time numbered in the hundreds, are blessed as they dock.

The vessel Cape Cod receives her blessing.

84 ST. PETER'S FIESTA

Photos courtesy of Gloucester Daily Times

The Blessing of the Fleet is performed on Stacy Boulevard in front of the Fisherman's Memorial, as boats gather in the harbor.

Fishing vessels dress for the occasion. Above, the St. Peter III hosts family and friends with a boat ride. Boat parties often included delicious foods such as baked-stuffed lobster and shrimp, prepared by the fishermen's wives.

Photo courtesy of Gloucester Daily Times

During the blessing, the names of boats are called out, one by one—and suddenly, the event becomes personalized, each name having personal meaning for each family of the fishing community, and for recreational boaters as well. Below and right, members of the community express their appreciation.

Photo courtesy of Gloucester Daily Times

Photos courtesy of Gloucester Daily Times

The Blessing has been performed through the years by several religious dignitaries.

Opposite, the blessing of 1968.

Nina Conti has opened her home to many religious dignitaries who have participated in the Blessing of the Fleet. Here she aids Cardinal Mederos for the event.

The Most Rev. Charles P. Greco, Bishop of Alexandria, Louisiana, shown here with Nina Conti during one of his many Fiesta visits. When offered a bounty of specially prepared Sicilian foods, the Bishop asks for only cherries. Here, Mrs. Conti happily obliges.

On the front porch of the Conti home on Stacy Boulevard: Tom Linquata, Nina Conti, The Bishop, Paul Conti, and Father Buecler.

Crowds gather for the blessing on Stacy Boulevard. Although today the Gloucester fishing fleet has dwindled, the blessing is also a time to reflect, remembering and honoring those who have lost their lives at sea.

FIESTA EVENTS

THE EVENTS that draw huge crowds during Fiesta are where hard work and hard play are intertwined. High-spirited, costumed revelers use their skill and experience to make their way along a grease-covered pole, capturing the bright red flag and the glory that goes right along with it. Crews of men test their strength and determination when the traditional Seine Boat Races take place off of Pavillion Beach. For years "colorful characters of the waterfront" have been entertaining the masses on the beach with their sheer exuberance, continuing these time-honored events that make the St. Peter's Fiesta so unique.

Photo courtesy of Gloucester Daily Times

THE GREASY POLE

Competitive walking or climbing a pole has roots in Italian history dating back to the year 1350. Gloucester's version of the "Greasy Pole" has been part of the Fiesta almost from the beginning.

The contest takes place on a platform located 200 yards off Pavillion Beach. Depending on the tide, the pole, which measures 35 to 40 feet in length, is approximately 40 feet above the surface of the water. After a thick application of industrial (and biodegradable) grease is applied to the walking surface, a red flag is nailed to the end of the pole. Young men risk bumps, brusies, and even cracked ribs for the opportunity to claim the flag, and the bragging rights that go with it.

The Greasy Pole competition is held twice during the Fiesta weekend. Saturday's contest is for those lucky enough to get their names on the select list of walkers. The Sunday competition is for the previous day's winner, past champions, and the designated progeny of retired champions. A Sunday champ can walk until he retires, at which time he will pick a younger walker to represent him on the pole. The winner is carried triumphantly back to shore on the shoulders of his friends, and receives a small cash prize, substantial bragging rights ,and the title of "champion" to wear proudly for the rest of his life.

Above, pole winner Jerome Liacano is carried on the shoulders of his peers, after the traditonal swim back to shore in the 1940's. Opposite, his son-in-law John (Beanie) Nicastro wins bragging rights in 1950, and later his grandson Paul Nicastro goes for it in 1984.

St. Peter's Fiesta Greasy Pole Winners

1931	SUN	Oritano Vincenzo	MON	Oritano Vincenzo
1932	SUN	Oritano Vincenzo	MON	Oritano Vincenzo
1933	SUN	Geronimo Parisi	MON	Geronimo Parisi
1934	SUN	Jimmy Sinagra	MON	Dominic Grillo
1935	SUN	Natale Misuraca	MON	cancelled - low tide
1936	SUN	Tom "Pee Wee" Randazza	MON	Jimmy Sinagra
1937	SUN	Tom "Pee Wee" Randazza	MON	Natale Misuraca
1938	SUN	Gerome Loicano	MON	cancelled - low tide
1939	SUN	Jerome Loicano	MON	Sammy Pecker Randazza
1940-45		No Fiesta - WWII		
1946	SUN	Joe Marino	MON	Joe Marino
1947	SUN	Jerome Loicano	MON	Joe Black Frontiero
1948	SUN	Peter Mione	MON	Joe Verga
1949	SUN	Louie Linquata	MON	Joe Agrusso
1950	SAT	Johnny Randazza	SUN	Jerome Loicano
1951	SAT	Gino Biondo	SUN	Louie Linquata
1952	SAT	Joe Agrusso	SUN	cancelled - rain
1953	SAT	Tommy Misuraca	SUN	Tommy Misuraca
1954	SAT	Johnny Quince	SUN	Tommy Misuraca
1955	SAT	John "Beanie" Nicastro	SUN	John "Beanie" Nicastro
1956	SAT	Carlo "Sleepy" Pallazolla	SUN	Carlo "Sleepy" Pallazolla
1957	SAT	John Frontiero	SUN	unknown
1958	SAT	Joe Black Frontiero	SUN	Mike Calomo
1959	SAT	Frank Catania	SUN	Phil Curcuru
1960	SAT	Phil Curcuru	SUN	Frank Benson
1961		No greasy pole due to storm damage to platform		
1962	SAT	Phil Curcuru	SUN	Phil Curcuru (cousin)
1963	SAT	Salvatore Testaverde	SUN	Joe Black Frontiero
1964	SAT	Phil Parisi	SUN	Phil Curcuru
1965	SAT	Phil Curcuru	SUN	Salvatore Russo
1966	SAT	Tom Wolfman Cavanaugh	SUN	Tom Wolfman Cavanaugh

Above, "Sleepy" Palazola relaxes on the beach after winning in 1956.

Right, a group celebrates a victory in a very early pole contest. Right, Joe Marino in 1946.

Opposite, this rare photograph of one of the first Greasy Pole contests in 1931 shows "Red" Curcuru falling from a pole that was located off the playground area of the Fort. The pole was later moved to a platform 200 yards from the beach.

FIESTA EVENTS 101

Photo courtesy of Gloucester Daily Times

St. Peter's Fiesta Greasy Pole Winners

1967	SAT	Salvy Benson	SUN	Vito Calamo
1968	SAT	Salvy Benson	SUN	Salvy Benson
1969	SAT	Salvy Benson	SUN	Gaetano Carini
1970	SAT	Gaetano Carini	SUN	Pat Palmisano
1971	SAT	Salvy Benson	SUN	Salvy Benson
1972	SAT	Tom Wolfman Cavanaugh	SUN	Salvy Benson (held on barge - platform damage)
1973	SAT	Tom Wolfman	SUN	Salvy Benson

(1973 - first woman to walk pole, Katrina Resevic)

1974	SAT	Tom Wolfman	SUN	Salvy Benson
1975	SAT	Anthony Matza Giambanco	SUN	Anthony Matza Giambanco
1976	SAT	Gaetano Carini	SUN	Benny Interante
1977	SAT	Billy Lumbruno	SUN	Anthony Matza Giambanco
1978	SAT	Bobby Brother Agostini	SUN	Anthony Matza Giambanco
1979	SAT	Joe Palmisano	SUN	Salvy Benson
1980	SAT	Paul Bertolino	SUN	Anthony Matza Giambanco
1981	SAT	Jerry Santuccio	SUN	Dom Verga
1982	SAT	Steve Stubby Asaro	SUN	Dom Verga
1983	SAT	Phil Verga	SUN	Jerry Santuccio
1984	SAT	Paul Nicastro	SUN	Peter Frontiero
1985	SAT	Tom Favazza	SUN	Dom Verga
1986	SAT	Jerry Ciolino	SUN	Scott Clayton
1987	SAT	Samo Frontiero	SUN	Peter Frontiero
1988	SAT	Anthony Saputo	SUN	Peter Frontiero

(1985 champ in Terrasini, Sicily)

Clockwise from right: Sal Scola, Naz Sanfillipo, winner Benny Interante, and Joe Biondo in 1976. Steve LaBlanc makes a clean grab. Scott Clayton celebrates victory on Pavillion Beach in 1986.

Opposite, the envy of any professional ballet dancer, Jerry Cioleno takes a dive.

Photo courtesy of Gloucester Daily Times

Lennie Biondo (right) slathers it on in 1991. Below, Lou Biondo slides off in 1986. A grease-covered Mitch McGillviray surfaces in 1987.

Opposite, "Busty" Palazola and Larry Randazza grease the pole for the 1972 contest.

Photos courtesy of Gloucester Daily Times

104   ST. PETER'S FIESTA

Photo courtesy of Gloucester Daily Times

St. Peter's Fiesta Greasy Pole Winners

1989	SAT	Russell Hines	SUN	Peter Frontiero
1990	SAT	Johnny Corollo	SUN	Peter Frontiero
1991	SAT	Jerry Cusamano	SUN	Peter Frontiero
1992	SAT	Nico Brancaleone	SUN	Peter Frontiero
1993	SAT	Steve LeBlanc	SUN	Peter Frontiero
1994	SAT	Dave Foote	SUN	Steve LeBlanc
1995	SAT	Steve Gray	SUN	Chris Carlson
1996	SAT	John Parisi	SUN	Rich Hopkins
1997	SAT	Shawn Porper	SUN	Rich Hopkins
1998	SAT	Jason Puglisi	SUN	Nino Sanfilippo
1999	FRI	Jake Wood (first year of Friday's Greasy Pole contest)		
	SAT	Jake Wood	SUN	Jake Wood
2000	FRI	Steve Decoste		
	SAT	Judd LaFlame	SUN	Samo Frontiero

Photos courtesy of Gloucester Daily Times

Salvi Benson, a twelve-time winner, shows how it's done.

Opposite, Salvi celebrates with, (left to right) Mitch McGillviray, Frank Frontiero, Bobby "Brother" Agostini, Dan Balbo, Mike Mitchell, and Samo Frontiero.

Photo courtesy of Gloucester Daily Times

St. Peter's Fiesta Winning Brothers Combinations

Nat Misuraca
 1935 SAT
 1937 MON

Mike Calomo
 1958 SUN

Salvy Benson
 1968 SAT & SUN
 1969 SAT
 1971 SAT & SUN
 1972 SUN
 1973 SAT & SUN
 1974 SAT & SUN
 1979 SUN

Tom Misuraca
 1953 SAT & SUN
 1954 SUN

Vito Calomo
 1967 SUN

Frank Benson
 1960 SUN

Pat Palmisano
 1970 SUN

Dom Verga
 1981 SUN
 1982 SUN
 1985 SUN

Joe Palmisano
 1979 SAT

Phil Verga
 1983 SAT

FIESTA EVENTS

Photo courtesy of Gloucester Daily Times

Above, in Indian headdress, brave Andrew Bertolino takes a fall. Walking the pole in costume has become a traditon over the years.

Pictured at left are Anthony Saputo, Anthony "Matza" Giambanco, Chris Carlson, Tom Abbott, Jerry Cilion, Mike Cusomano, and Joe Calomo.

Photo courtesy of Gloucester Daily Times

Jack Linquata, above, hams it up for the camera before a pole contest. Right, the ultimate Greasy Pole fashion statement.

FIESTA EVENTS 109

Photos courtesy of Gloucester Daily Times

Above, Michael Linquata makes a flying attempt in 1978. Tommy Favazza, right, seems to defy gravity.

Opposite, the traditonal victory swim back to shore in 1978. Pictured are: winner, "Brother" Agostini, Gus Sanfillipo, Bobby Palozolo, Joe Palmisano, and Wayne Ciarametaro.

Clockwise from right: Johnny Parisi reaches for the flag. Rich Hopkins, a 2-time winner, makes it look all too easy. Peter Frontiero wins in 1984, his first of eight victories.

Opposite, Joey Palmisano slides his way to victory in 1979.

Photos courtesy of Gloucester Daily Times

Winning Father and Son Combinations

Joe Black Frontiero
 1958 SAT
 1963 SUN

Peter Black Frontiero
 1984 SUN
 1987 SUN
 1988 SUN
 1989 SUN
 1990 SUN
 1991 SUN
 1992 SUN
 1993 SUN

John Beanie Nicastro
 1955 SAT & SUN

Paul Nicastro
 1984 SAT

Winning Father, Son, and Grandson Combinations

Jerome Loicano
 1938 SUN
 1939 SUN
 1947 SUN
 1950 SUN

John Beanie Nicastro
 1955 SAT & SUN

Paul Nicastro (grandson)
 1984 SAT

Photos courtesy of Gloucester Daily Times

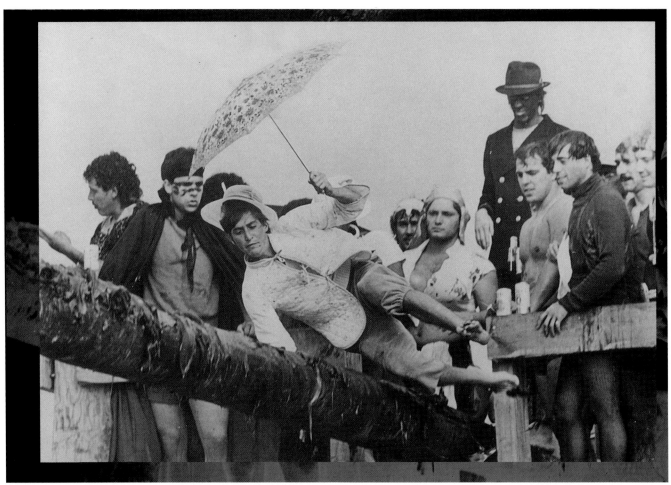
Photo courtesy of Gloucester Daily Times

Photo courtesy of Gloucester Daily Times

Above, taking notes on the strategy of Sam Frontiero are (left to right): Peter Frontiero, Sal Corrllio, Paul Bertolino, Mick Verga, and Steve Goulart. Sam's strategy pays off, as he rejoices with his competitors.

Opposite, top, Tom Lupo does a balancing act. On the platform are (left to right), Frank Gentile, Tom Lupo, Mike Novello, David Quinn, Joe Tumbiolo, and Jimmy Verga.

Opposite, bottom, Johnny Corello finds his way to the end of the pole, and is carried to shore by Matty Randazza and Jo-jo Sanfolipo.

FIESTA EVENTS 115

Clockwise from top left, a stauesque Anthony "Matza" Giambanca stands effortlessly in 1980. Albert Genovese, Matza Giambanca, and Steve Lapeen celebrate. Matza is carried in by (left to right), Dom Verga, Joe Palmisano, Jack Linquata, Anthony Millitello, Steve Lapine, and Jerry Ciliono.

Photos courtesy of Gloucester Daily Times

Left, Peter Frontiero makes a great grab. Below, Larry Biondo looses seems to have things under control, but ultimately bottoms out.

Photos courtesy of Gloucester Daily Times

FIESTA EVENTS 117

Photos courtesy of Gloucester Daily Times

Fiesta competition doesn't stop at the end of the Greasy Pole. Clockwise from top left, the traditonal watermelon-eating contest. Tony D'Antonio wears blueberry pie in a 1988 pie-eating contest. Joe Palmisano keeps the little ones in line in 1991.

Clockwise from top, children participate in an old-fashioned sack race. This Mexican tradition gets a New England twist, breaking the piñata with an oar. Children delight in a carnival ride by the sea.

Photos courtesy of Gloucester Daily Times

FIESTA EVENTS

THE SEINE BOAT RACES

Seine boat racing is a highlight of the Fiesta sporting activities dating back to the first citywide celebration ever held in Gloucester.

Purse seine fishing was a common method of fishing during the early decades of the Fiesta. Fish were captured in large floatiing nets and then "pursed up" along side the seine boat, then loaded onto the larger fishing vessel. When the larger boat had reached its capacity, it then returned to port.

Since most of Gloucester's fishing fleet stayed in port during the Fiesta, the seine boats were available for competitive racing. Large enough to hold most of the crew of a fishing boat, the seine boats were used to settle race challenges issued between boat crews, each boasting the best and strongest men in the fleet.

The seine boat races take place on the waters of Gloucester Harbor, off of Pavillion Beach. Junior and Senior divisions compete in the preliminary heats prior to Sunday's big race. Crews in each of the three boats—the Nina, Pinta, and Santa Maria—must row to its own flag anchored one-half mile off shore. After making the crucial turn, they must then race back to the beach. The first boat to hit the sand of Pavillion Beach is declared the winner, and is awarded an American flag. Second place finishers are awarded the Italian flag.

Above, seine boats at work in 1931. This hard-working crew was the first to win a seine boat race. The name of this crew was "Hoopla."

Opposite, the calm, sun-dappled waters of Gloucester Harbor contrast with the intense efforts of two crews as they race back to shore in 1980.

St. Peter's Fiesta Seine Boat Winners

1931	SUN	Hoopla	MON	Hoopla
1932	SUN	Hoopla	MON	Hoopla
1933	SUN	Capt. Drum	MON	Capt. Drum
1934	SUN	Capt. Drum	MON	Capt. Drum (defeated U.S.S. Tenn team)
1935	SUN	The Salvatore	MON	The Natale II
1936	SUN	Marietta & Mary	MON	Capt. Drum
1937	SUN	Antonina	MON	Antonina
1938	SUN	Balilla	MON	Antonina
1939	SUN	The Salvatore	MON	Antonina
1940-45		No Fiesta due to WWII		
1946	SUN	Antonina	MON	Antonina
1947	SUN	Eleanor	MON	Famiglia
1948	SUN	Jennie & Lucia	MON	Nyoda
1949	SUN	The Alden	MON	The Jackie B.
1950	SAT	unknown	SUN	Santa Maria
1951	SAT	Alden	SUN	Alden
1952	SUN	Nina (new seine boat)		
1953	SUN	Nina (Capt. Sal Nicastro)		
1954	SUN	Nina (Capt. Jim Verga)		
1955	SUN	Nina (Joe Parisi & Tom Linquata)		
1956	SUN	Santa Maria		
1957	SUN	unknown		
1958	SUN	Renegades		
1959	SUN	Renegades		
1960	SUN	Beachcombers		
1961	SUN	Vagabonds		
1962	SUN	Beachcombers		
1963	SUN	Troublemakers		
1964	SUN	Gondoliers		

Above, early seine boat races.

Opposite, top left, this 1934 seine boat crew included oarsmen: Jack Agrusso (Captain), Peter Mione (coach), Tony Alow, Iscidor Tarentino, Steve Carbone, Bastiano Seina, Joseph Chiametaro, Sam Irato, Joseph Billante, and Frank Consigilo. The seine boat crew on the right were the winners in 1935.

President of the Fiesta Committee, Tom Brancleone recognizes Nino Lafata as one of the first seine boat rowers. The photos on the opposite page show Laffatta on the bow, as he celebrates the win with his crew "Hoopla" in 1931.

Below, the faces behind the voices that have provided great play-by-play throughout the years. Pictured from left to right are announcers Sam Nicastro, Tom Brancaleone, Michael DiLaberti, and Sammy "Logie" Frontiero.

FIESTA EVENTS **125**

Crowds gather to watch the blindman dory race, where blindfolded crews try and make their way back to shore.

Above, "The Gondoliers," winners in 1964. Pictured from left to right are Peter Mocerie, Joe Orlando, Steve Cambria, Busty Moceri, Carlo Moceri, Sam Lagrasso, Carlo Ciolino, Tom Brancelone, Joe Orlando, and Nino Sanfillipo. Below, claiming the flag by day, and dressed to the nines by night at the awards ceremony.

FIESTA EVENTS 127

Above, seine boats approach the flag at the halfway point in 1964.

Left, a 1975 crew feels the burn. Pictured from front to back, left row: Joe Biondo, Peter Asaro, Joe Capone, and Dan Balbo; right row: John Decaro, Andrew Bonina, Sal Sanfillipo, Naz San, and mascots Joe Palmisano and Larry Biondo.

Opposite, the thrill of victoy and the agony of defeat are epitomized at the end of this race in 1977.

Photo courtesy of Gloucester Daily Times

St. Peter's Fiesta Seine Boat Winners

1965 SUN Gondoliers	1977 SUN The Kids	1989 SUN Raging Bulls
1966 SUN Young at Heart	1978 SUN Mean Machine	1990 SUN The Stoppers
1967 SUN Youngsters	1979 SUN (The Race) Renegades & Mean Machine	1991 SUN Allied Forces
1968 SUN Youngsters		1992 SUN Allied Forces
1969 SUN Vagabonds	1980 SUN The Kids	1993 SUN Over The Top
1970 SUN Young Scrods	1981 SUN The Kids	1994 SUN Determination
1971 SUN Youngsters	1982 SUN The Kids	1995 SUN Determination
1972 SUN All Beefers	1983 SUN Desire	1996 SUN Die Hard
1973 SUN 3-way tie	1984 SUN Desire	1997 SUN Die Hard
1974 SUN All Beefers	1985 SUN Desire	1998 SUN Stayin' Alive
1975 no winner due to oar selection dispute	1986 SUN Desire	1999 SUN Perfect Storm
	1987 SUN Raging Bulls	2000 SUN Koa's
1976 SUN Dirty Dozen	1988 SUN Raging Bulls	

FIESTA EVENTS

Photos courtesy of Gloucester Daily Times

Spectators brave the weather, as Fiesta events take place rain or shine.

Below, an excruciating effort in 1980—pictured are, from left to right, Scott Phinney, Phil Francie, Dave Rose, Scott Morrisey, Frank Damico, Mo Montgomery, Dave Corrico, and Joey Borge, (obscured) Ed Vannah, Tom Carrerio.

Opposite, top, seine boats slice through the water. Bottom, a crew performs the intense "depth charge"—the last 10 strokes of the race.

Photo courtesy of Gloucester Daily Times

Above, Junior seine boat crew "Young Bloods" pull together in 1978.

Left, another junior crew, "The Terminators," wave their victory flag.

Andy Orlando and "Sleepy" Palazola celebrate as their crew are first to hit the beach.

Below, the crew poses for a victory mug: left to right, Scott Phinney, Jack Anderson, Mike Clay (bottom left), Jim Tarantino, tom Bammarito, Joe Comenelli, Phil Parisi, Steve Goodick, Steve Moore (under flag), Tony Frontiero, Andy Orlando, and "Sleepy" Palazola.

FACES IN THE CROWD

THE FACE of the St. Peter's Fiesta is ageless. It reflects the efforts of those who orchestrate the daunting details behind the scenes—it reflects the pride of the participants, and the joy of the spectators. Fiesta will continue to delight the senses for years to come. The sights and sounds, the tastes and aromas, are as familiar to this community as the smile of an old friend. The Sicilian and Portugese communities have extended the richness of their heritage throughout the years, touching all who come to the Fiesta.

Clockwise from top left: Nina Randazza and Maria Favazza 1953; Grace Pasquali, Katie Foote, Capt. Salvatore Favazza, Rosie Verga, Pimie Biondo, 1952; Peter Favazza and Capt. Salvatore Favazza; Pearl Parisi, Kathleen Giamanco, Agnes Burnham, Grace Pasquali; Josina Machi dances with her son Joe in 1980.

Opposite, band leader Victor Childers conducts the St. Ann's Church band in 1962.

Above, Fiesta Committee members of 1977 (from left to right) Carlos Moceri, Santo Militello, Nick Novello, Joe Kyrouz, Gaspar Lafata, Sam Linquata, and Sam Militello.

Right, Fiesta dignitaries with then Governor Endicott Peabod.

Opposite, clockwise from top left: a waiting for the parade; a group photo from the 1950's; Governor Mike Dukakis and Sam Linquata; local police join a family for a Fiesta picnic in the "Fort" neighborhood; carrying the statue in the late 1980's, left to right, Peter Frontiero, Sam Militello, Larry Sabato, and Sam Linquata.

Clockwise from left: Sandy Favazza, Ralph B. O'Maley, Benny Curcuru, unknown, Govenor Endicott Peabody, and Dave Harrison; the St. Peter's Auxillary.

Opposite, clockwise from top left: Grace and Philip Parisi; a grand display in the "Fort" neighborhood; waiting for the parade; Anthony Gallo, brothers Dominic and Joe Novello, and Ben Favazza; cutting a rug in 1981; fierce pie-eating competition.

A dedication to long-time committee member Joe Kyrouz, in appreciation to his many contributions to the St. Peter's Fiesta.

Ever since I could remember, Fiesta was a big part of my life. During this time, my dad, Joe Kyrouz, became so busy with trying to fit in time for Fiesta meetings while running his friendly grocery business. It is with great pleasure that I tell a story which reflects and commemorates some Fiesta memories that are held in high regards in the hearts of my entire family.

A typical Fiesta for us would include meeting the Cardinal who visited for the blessing and opening Mass on the Sunday morning. Since dad was religious chairperson, we had this special privilege.

A long time ago when my cousins and I were young children, we used to be at my grandma Grace Parisi's, who lived on Beach Court. There we would gather with all of our relatives to eat wonderful, traditional Italian foods—and boy there was plenty of it for anyone who walked in from off the street.

My grandfather, Philip Parisi, was one of the original fishing captains who would dress all in white and march down the street in the procession or parade, strutting proud along with his peers.

Occasionally, something new was added or changed to the Fiesta. People of all walks of life, race, and nationality could join in the celebration.

It is with great pride and joy that I remember my own dad marching down the street with his fellow committee men—my family and I snapping as many pictures as we could. Many people today still do not realize that my dad was not Italian, but in fact, Lebanese, and full-blooded, I might add. My father's people, the Kyrouz's, were so proud of one another and supported dad in his involvement with Fiesta.

As little children, we all participated in the parade and couldn't wait for all the games and dances at the corner as well as the different contests which were held all during Fiesta.

Fiesta really hit home for my family, as we shall never forget all the great times and our pillar of strength, which was our dad, Joe Kyrouz. We know that his spirit is with us and is something we hold deep in our hearts.

Our city of Gloucester has always lived up to it's reputation of being very hospitable. Our families come first, traditions are passed on. The St. Peter's Fiesta will always be a main event to this community for years to come. It is with the utmost respect and reverence that we pay tribute to all those people young and old who made the Fiesta what it is today.

—Cecilia Kyrouz Doucette

Fiesta 2000 has now come and gone, another one for the history books. But this year was just a little different in my opinion, for a number of reasons. It was as if I went back in time for a brief moment, going back to the old days of living down the Fort. This time of year everyone seems to come out of the woodwork, you see people you have not seen in years, and it brings back great memories. And some great feelings of pride of my Italian heritage, and to be part of growing up down the Fort.

As the weekend drew closer, more people were coming to town and the Buzz was in the air, my brother came in, I did get to see him for at least two hours before everyone else did. Cousins, old friends, the people you wanted to see, and the people you did not want to see. As you looked around you saw a lot of people from the old Fort Gang, and people who had strong ties with that part of town. Some things never change in Gloucester but maybe they shouldn't—that's what gives Gloucester it's character.

It was now Fiesta Sunday the biggest day of the four day event, my seine boat crew (KAOS), and I were preparing for the big race, which no one gave us a chance of winning. Our blood was pumping and we had a good feeling about today. Some friends stopped by to wish us luck as they did to the other crews.

When we got to the beach we were ready, we were pumped, and no one was going to stop us. Off we went to a great start, and we did not look back, as we got closer to the beach you could hear the screams getting closer and closer. As was passed the Greasy Pole the adrenaline kicked in and we knew it was ours. Everyone pulling together like a well-oiled machine. We hit the beach in victory, and the American Flag was placed on our boat. I was proud and happy as I could be, winning a race that takes every ounce of energy that you have—combine that with the crowd and tradition of the Fiesta and a bunch of guys that gave everything they had for seven and half minutes. My heart was pounding with pride.

As I turned to the crowd, I saw all the gang on the beach cheering and running to shake hands to congratulate us. It was at that moment that you were glad you grew up in Gloucester, It was a very good feeling.

But it was not over, it was time for the Greasy Pole, it was part of my agreement to row, after we won that I get a victory ride to the pole. After twenty years of walking the Greasy Pole I was walking on a cloud as I sat on the platform, thinking of winning two flags in one day. Which was not to be, after four rounds of walking, my cousin Sam Frontiero leaned over to me and said he was nervous to be out there today, that may be a good omen. Because two minutes later he was the Greasy Pole Champ 2000.

That was not the end, everyone on that pole was very excited that Samo won, one for the old guys, one for the old Fort Gang, it was a good thing to happen to a great guy. As we hit the beach with the new champ, we looked up and saw the old gang on the beach chanting "Samo, Samo, Samo!" There must have been 25 or more that came to together to cheer on one of their own. We carried Sam down Beach Court as the tradition goes, we stopped half way to put him down because he could not believe he won. At that point something happened that I have not seen in a long time when it comes to Greasy Pole walkers, all the veterans had tears in their eyes—Matza Giambanco, Anthony Saputo, Joe Palmisano and me, plus other family and friends who know how much it means. Not just to grab the flag, but tradition, family, pride in our heritage. When people say what is the big deal about this pole walk, they have no idea what it really means.

Seventy-five years ago when my grandfather and other relative started the Fiesta, they had no idea what it would turn into, I am sure they must be looking down on this with big smiles on their faces. To see that their son and daughters, grandchildren, and great-grandchildren and a town have kept it going for so long.

To people, the Fiesta is just another excuse to party, to others it's a big traffic jam, or inconvenience. If they knew what it was really about, I believe more people would enjoy the Fiesta. I hope the tradition lasts for many years to come.

—Thomas Favazza
Air Guitar Champ 1985
Greasy Pole Champ 1985
Seine Boat Camp 2000

Story posted in the *Gloucester Daily Times*, August 2, 2000

DEDICATION

In loving memory of Captain Salvatore Favazza